BOARD
MEETINGS

A Guide for Charter Schools

Marci Cornell-Feist

Fourth Printing, May 2015

Graphic Design by Kerry Kenneally, www.kerrykenneally.com.
For more information, contact BoardOnTrack at www.boardontrack.com.

CONTENTS

INTRODUCTION:

What Makes Meetings Effective?

This guide is based on the practices of some of the most effective charter school boards, yielding the best student achievement results in the country. Since the mid 1990s, I have worked with hundreds of charter school boards nationwide and attended countless board meetings. There is a direct correlation between how a board approaches its meetings and how effective it is at implementing its strategic vision for increasing student achievement.

Highly effective boards do a fair amount of work in between board meetings by harnessing the energy of committees. But, the real formal work of the collective board happens during the regularly scheduled board meetings. Having sat through hundreds of charter school board meetings, I am often struck by how groups of incredibly smart, dynamic individuals can have some of the dullest meetings on the planet. Why is this, when most charter schools have plenty of pressing strategic issues to discuss? The keys to successful board meetings involve:

1. Preparation. Agendas are developed and meeting documents are provided in advance.

2. Presentation. Discussion is organized and productive.

3. Strategy. Meetings focus on advancing the board's goals and priorities, rather than only reacting to the latest challenges.

This book answers the most commonly asked questions about charter school board meetings. Making your meetings dynamic and focused is the best way to retain exceptional board members. Effective board meetings are critical in accomplishing your board's goals.

How to Use This Book

Part I features some of the most common, most important questions I've been asked in my twenty years of working with charter school boards. These are organized by topic and listed in the table of contents.

Part II features various samples that illustrate some of the recommendations described here. Feel free to customize them as needed. There are also quizzes for your board to take.

Four icons help you find more information.

Ⅱ indicates that there is a sample in part II of this book.

🖥 indicates that there are digital versions available at www.boardontrack.com, which you can customize.

🍂 indicates that BoardOnTrack offers an electronic tool that helps facilitate this process.

⚖ indicates that laws, particularly open meeting laws, likely apply to this topic, and they can differ significantly from state to state. Be sure to confirm with your legal counsel before acting on this type of issue.

PART I. Q & A

1. Scheduling

1.1. How often should a charter school board meet?

A charter school board, particularly in its first five years, should meet at least once a month, or at a minimum, ten times a year. During the startup (pre-opening phase), it may be necessary to meet twice a month. Once the school is open, the full board should not have to meet more than once a month, unless there is an unusual situation.

Another good reason for charter school boards to meet frequently is to maintain transparency. Charter schools are public schools and are primarily supported by taxpayer dollars. To secure the public trust, charter schools should make it as easy as possible for the broader community to see what decisions are being made.

BEST PRACTICE TIP

Why Every Month?

Many charter school board members feel that meeting monthly seems too time-consuming, and fear that potential board members will be too busy to make this kind of commitment. They therefore suggest meeting every other month.

Meeting once every two months is not enough to govern effectively. Board members should only serve if they can make a sufficient commitment to complete the board's business, and this means monthly meetings for most charter schools.

The board holds and is responsible for the school's charter and is ultimately accountable to the authorizer and the community to deliver exceptional results. There are too many critical, policy-level decisions that need to be made, particularly in the first few years of the charter, for the board to hold fewer than ten meetings a year.

1.2. How long should our board meetings be?

Board meetings should rarely exceed two hours. If your board meetings routinely run longer than two hours, you are doing something wrong: not harnessing the power of committees to distill critical information for the full board, focusing on too much detail, not giving advanced readings to frame the discussion, or simply not sticking to your agenda. With careful preparation and a focus on the strategic, your meetings should not exceed two hours.

BEST PRACTICE TIP

If Two Hours Are Not Enough

If your board is having difficulty completing its work within two hours, try shifting from an early evening meeting to an early morning meeting. When board members need to get to work on time, they tend to do a better job of sticking to the agenda.

1.3. How should we create a board meeting calendar?

Annually, you should clarify the time commitment expected of the board members by creating a calendar that shows all the board's activities and events. This will help you achieve better attendance at board meetings and keep the board on track towards working on its priorities. To create a schedule your board is likely to stick to, consider the following questions and processes:

- **Revisit the time of day for the meetings.** Are evenings still convenient? Would you have more luck getting trustees to attend if the meetings were in the early morning?

- **Revisit the day of the week.** Is the standing day still a good fit for the majority of trustees? Should you meet on a different day?

- **Next, sketch out the significant milestones for the year.** You can complete this exercise as a group—it can serve as a great board education exercise—or have a smaller group (committee chairs and the CEO) take a stab at a draft and then seek input from the rest of the board.

    CEO: *The staff member at the top of the organizational chart, ultimately in charge. Other names for this position include school leader, school director, principal, headmaster, head of school, and executive director. The term "CEO" evokes the business responsibilities of this position, such as oversight of fiscal and organizational systems, which requires the equivalent of a CEO of a multi-million dollar enterprise, as well as responsibilities of academic oversight.*

The exercise:

1. Hang up twelve pieces of flip-chart paper around the room.

2. Write the name of each month of the year on one of the pieces of flip chart paper.

3. Start with the area of the board's work that is the most time bound—finances.

4. Try mapping backwards: What month will you approve the final budget? Write that down. This means that the month before, you

should write down "discuss final draft budget;" the month before that, you should discuss the basic financial model, etc.

5.   Take all of the key topics, and plot them out month by month.

This will give you a clear sketch of the main topics you will need to cover at each month's board meetings.

If some months look overloaded, see if you can move around the timing for some of the key tasks. Some tasks tend to be very time bound, others are more flexible.

In addition, seeing all the work necessary will help settle the question, "Do we really need to meet every month?"

Then for extra bonus points, ask yourselves, "What are the big strategic issues we need to discuss? When will we have time to discuss these issues?" Try to find some months when you can shrink the basic board business time and free some time up for deeper strategic discussions.

📖 *Sample on page 42*

1.4. How often should we have a board retreat?

Board Retreat: A special board meeting, outside your regular schedule, where the board focuses on strategic vision, team building, and other issues besides the regular business at hand. Retreats are often held offsite and commonly run by an outside facilitator.

It is highly recommended that the board have a retreat once a year. Typically, the purpose of the retreat should be to take stock of the previous year and plan the work of the board for the upcoming year.

In addition, most boards find it useful to block off two or three deeper strategy sessions during the year.

BEST PRACTICE TIP

Making Time for Strategy

You might find it useful to shorten the "board business" at every other meeting, reserving larger chunks of time on the agendas for deeper strategy discussions.

2. Meeting Materials: Agendas, Minutes, and Supporting Documents

2.1. Who should create the board meeting agenda?

The agenda should be created by the board chair and the CEO well in advance of each meeting. Ideally within 48 hours after the completion of a board meeting, the board chair and CEO should debrief the previous board meeting and draft the agenda for the next meeting. Planning the agenda far in advance will help ensure that the meeting's content focuses on the strategic, not the reactive.

Board Meeting Preparation Cycle

When	What
Day after previous meeting	Board chair and CEO debrief and draft agenda for next meeting
4 Weeks Before Meeting	Draft agenda sent to full board and committee chairs
3 Weeks Before Meeting	Comments incorporated and agenda finalized
1 Week Before Meeting	Committee reports finalized and advanced board meeting packet sent
Week of Meeting	Full board reads all advanced material and is ready to discuss strategy

Sample on page 38

2.2. What should a board meeting agenda look like?

- The board should use a consistent agenda format.

- The most important items on the agenda should be addressed first. People will be most attentive at the beginning of the meeting. Also if you do housekeeping at the beginning, it can encourage tardiness. If people feel like they would miss something important when they are late, they are more likely to come on time. Routine matters should be covered toward the end of the meeting.

- Each agenda item should be numbered.

- Next to each agenda item, state the number of minutes this discussion will take. In addition, the agenda should indicate the purpose of including each agenda item, such as "for board action," "vote," "for providing information," "to get the board's perspective," and so forth.

- Last-minute additions to the agenda should be discouraged. It is rarely good business to vote on something without prior notice or to introduce new business that is not on the agenda.

📖 *Sample on page 38*

BEST PRACTICE TIP

Agenda Item Cover Sheets

Consider using a cover/summary sheet for each agenda item. It provides:

- The purpose of the item's inclusion and relevant background

- A brief discussion of the item's context, such as why it is on the agenda and why it should be approved

- A summary of any previous discussion on the topic

- An indication of why the information is being presented—such as a request at a prior board meeting

- A recommendation regarding what outcome or action should be taken, worded as a draft motion or motions, if it is an action item. The language of the motion can be changed at the meeting, if necessary, following any discussion. For simple discussion or informational items, this would be left blank.

📖 *Sample on page 39* 🕖 *www.boardontrack.com*

2.3. What's the role of the full board in creating the board meeting agenda?

Ideally, the key topics for each meeting would have been mapped out in a strategic board calendar at the beginning of each year and approved by the full board.

Then, roughly a month before each board meeting, the board chair and the CEO should take a stab at creating a draft agenda. The draft agenda should be sent to the full board for comments well in advance of the meeting. Trustees should have a chance to weigh in if they feel something else should be on the agenda.

Ultimately, it should be up to the board chair and the CEO to make the final call about what is on the agenda.

BEST PRACTICE TIP

Agenda by Board Chair and CEO

The board chair and the CEO should use a team approach in designing the agenda. There should also be a procedure by which board members can submit items they would like to be considered for the upcoming agenda. Ideally, the board chair and CEO will have created and shared a draft board calendar for the entire year and will be preparing agendas from these prioritized items, not merely reacting to whatever is immediately in front of them.

Note: BoardOnTrack membership is a Web-based board platform that includes an online automated process to craft and submit draft agendas to the full board and to receive comments in a timely way.

 www.boardontrack.com

2.4. Are advance board packets really necessary? They seem like a lot of work.

> *Advance Packet: The set of documents that support issues to be discussed at a board or committee meeting, sent in advance of the meeting so that attendees can review them beforehand. The packet will include the agenda, minutes to be approved from the previous meeting, and any other documents to be distributed, such as agenda item summary sheets, committee reports, and so on.*

Yes, advance board packets are necessary. In order to have strategic, policy-level discussions at your board meetings, members need to be informed about the items that will be discussed, read relevant materials, and come to board meetings prepared to take the required actions. This can only happen if board packets are sent out in advance.

Too much valuable board meeting time is often wasted sharing basic facts and figures. This can all happen in advance in a board packet, saving valuable board meeting time for discussing strategy. It is the school staff's responsibility to assure that these packets are assembled and distributed in a timely way—at least several days in advance of the meeting.

BEST PRACTICE TIP

Distributing Advance Packets

Take a poll every year to find out how far in advance board members need to receive the advanced materials in order to come prepared for your board meetings. Make an agreement that all committees and senior staff will have their materials ready by the agreed upon time. Actively enforce the agreed upon timeline. Most effective boards send the packet electronically, in one e-mail rather than a flurry of e-mails, and avoid late breaking news or sending out last-minute documents. This will ensure that members have time to read the materials and will help you focus on the strategic, not the reactive.

Note: BoardOnTrack membership is a Web-based board platform that includes an online automated process to distribute board packets to the full board and to receive comments in a timely way.

 www.boardontrack.com

2.5. What should we do if people won't read the board materials in advance?

Discuss this as a group at a board meeting. Vote to agree to all read the materials in advance. Then at subsequent meetings, if trustees ask questions about things that were already spelled out in the advanced materials–don't answer them. Say, "That was covered in the advanced materials; remember, we all agreed to read them in advance." If a trustee chronically does not read the advance materials, then the board chair or chair of the Governance Committee should pull them aside and remind them that this is a requirement of board service. Time is too precious to waste on repeating things that were spelled out in the advanced reading materials. If a trustee consistently can't come prepared to board meetings, then you should consider removing them from the board.

It's interesting; charter schools are all about accountability. The whole premise of charter schools is that we are given a lot more freedom to operate in the manner we see fit, but with that freedom comes a great deal of accountability. Why would you not hold your board members to the same level of accountability that you hold the students and teachers at your school?

I know they are "only volunteers," but for better or worse, the board members are on the hook to govern a multi-million dollar public enterprise, so they should be held accountable for doing their homework before every board meeting.

> **Governance Committee:** *the committee that focuses on the health of the board, nominates new trustees, organizes board education, maps out succession planning for officers and trustees, and similar tasks to ensure that the board is functioning effectively.*

2.6. What should good minutes look like?

Meeting minutes are a formal recording of transactions that happened at a particular time and place. Minutes are a record of what was done at the meeting, *not* a detailed transcript of what was said by members. They are used for clarification of past activities and actions. Minutes help ensure continuity in the organization's transactions.

Meeting minutes are legal documents that auditors and other verifiers may review. They must be accurate and should never reflect the opinion of the secretary or minutes taker. They should be brief and easy to read. A separate paragraph should be used for each topic. It is useful to use bold type to identify each topic.

Minutes Format: The following should be recorded at the top of the minutes: the name of the organization, date, time, and location of the meeting. Note whether it is a special or regular meeting.

Additionally:

- List the full names of present and absent members. Note any guests who are in attendance.

- In the first paragraph, specify the time the meeting was convened and the name of the presiding officer. Record minutes in accordance with the order of events. Note the approval (and amendment) of the minutes of the previous meeting.

- Note the review and acceptance of the financial report.

- Briefly summarize the main points of discussions only if it sets precedent or is critical. Otherwise, simply note that discussion ensued.

- Indicate major problems stated and any suggestions proposed.

- Record conflicting points of view for clarification of action.

- Record all motions. Some organizations record the name of the individual who made the motion; it is not necessary to state the person seconding the motion.

- Record abstentions. State whether the motion failed or carried.

- Note the time of adjournment. End the minutes with the name of the recorder and the secretary who has reviewed the minutes.

Remember, minutes are a matter of public record and can be requested by a member of the general public at any time. Different states have varying open meeting laws, which vary in specific requirements. Be sure you understand your presiding law, in terms of what is required for minutes. These are general guidelines.

 Sample on page 40 *www.boardontrack.com*

BEST PRACTICE TIP

Posting Minutes Online

Consider posting your minutes on the school's website or in other easily accessible locations to keep constituents informed about the major decisions made at the meeting. However, first confirm that your board's posting practices conform to your state's open meeting law.

BoardOnTrack provides a way to take minutes online and post them to your school's website with a click of the mouse.

2.7. Do committees need to take meeting minutes?

Yes, it is important for each committee to keep accurate meeting minutes. The committee minutes should be a record of the actions that were taken at the meeting. Meeting minutes should be stored in a central location and backed up periodically. In addition, they should be distributed to the rest of the board, so that everyone can keep up to date with committee activities.

BoardOnTrack builds an institutional memory for you, helping you keep track of agendas, minutes, and associated board materials.

 www.boardontrack.com

2.8. What should committee minutes look like?

Your state's open meeting law may have specific requirements, but in general, committee minutes should be a very concise record of the actions that were taken by the committee. Specifically, they should include or list:

- The date, time, and location of the meeting

- All board members and senior staff that were in attendance

- Any guests that were present

- Any absences

- The time the meeting was called to order

- All actions that were taken, as succinctly as possible

- Agreed-upon "to dos"

- The time the meeting adjourned

2.9. Who should take the minutes?

The secretary of the board is responsible for ensuring that accurate minutes are taken at each board meeting. This *does not* mean that the secretary must take the minutes; he or she must ensure that it is done. It is not acceptable for the board chair, CEO, or senior staff to take the minutes.

 Sample on page 47

BEST PRACTICE TIP

Non-Board Members Taking Minutes

Find an outside person to take the minutes. This will allow all board members and senior staff to actively participate in the discussions. The board secretary may ask for a volunteer. Some charter schools have asked junior staff at local law firms to take the minutes, or college students needing to complete community service requirements. The board may also consider allocating a small amount of money to hire someone to take minutes. The secretary, however, should always review the minutes for accuracy.

3. Roles and Responsibilities

3.1. Who should be presenting at board meetings?

Any board member might present information to the full board. Let's face it, it's boring to sit through a two hour meeting with the same person doing all of the presenting! Yet that is how many charter school boards operate. The CEO does 90 percent of the talking/ presenting. This makes sense during the startup phase, when the founding leader has all of the information, the board has very little knowledge, and there is often late breaking news to report. But once the school is open, others should participate more actively.

An important sign that your board is making the necessary shift from a founding board to a sustainable governing board is the percent of time that board members present vs. the CEO.

As your organization matures, committee chairs should be presenting more and more of the relevant information.

3.2. Should committees report at every full board meeting?

Committees should provide written updates before every board meeting. These written reports should be sent out as part of the "board packet" of advance meeting material. There should be an expectation that every trustee will attend the meeting having read the materials.

There is no need for committees to make a presentation at every board meeting. They should only make a presentation if there is something strategic for the board to discuss.

Board meeting time should rarely be spent on discussing things that have happened in the past. Meetings should focus primarily on the future.

BEST PRACTICE TIP

Are You Focused Enough on Strategy?

Review your board meeting agendas from the past four to six board meetings. Mark next to each item what is reactive vs. strategic. Calculate how your board is doing compared to our gold standard. Then discuss your results as a group, and decide what you want to do about it.

Also, when you are creating annual board goals, delineate which goals are reactive and which are strategic. Aspire to reach a balance as shown below, based on your organization's stage of development.

Strategic, Not Reactive: Creating the Future

# Yrs Old	% Time Creating the Future	% Time Oversight Here and Now
5	90%	10%
4	80%	20%
3	60%	40%
2	40%	60%
1	20%	80%

3.3. Should we take attendance at our board meetings?

Yes. One of charter school boards' biggest stumbling blocks is dealing with unproductive board members. Attendance at board meetings is a key component of performance expectations for individual board members. When people agree to serve on the board, they must also agree to fulfill these expectations. The rest of the board has to hold each member accountable and be prepared to take action if someone does not follow through. The meeting minutes must include attendances and absences.

 Sample on page 40

BEST PRACTICE TIP

Attendance Chart on Minutes

Include an annual attendance chart with the monthly minutes. This is a simple way to show who routinely attends meetings and who does not, and build a sense of accountability.

3.4. How should we handle public comment at board meetings?

Some charter laws have specific language that spells out the requirements of public comment, but most do not. First, check the requirements of your state's law. If there are no specific requirements, then best practice shows us that you should do the following:

- Have a clearly stated and well-publicized public comment policy, outlined in a document that you can distribute at board meetings and to members of the public who wish to comment.

- Require that those who wish to speak at the board meeting submit a request in writing at least 24 hours in advance to the board chair.

- The board chair decides if it is appropriate for a comment to take place at the board meeting or if it is better suited for the management team to address first.

- Whether or not the comment is discussed at the board meeting, there should be clear, timely communication back to the member of the public who made the request.

⚖ 🏛 *Sample on page 53*

3.5. What role should the general public play at board meetings?

While few members of the general public might attend your board meetings, meetings are open, and you should be equipped to accommodate those who do attend. Provide them with a designated place to sit, away from the board table.

Your school should have a formal procedure for parents or others to follow should they want to speak at the board meeting. Often, this procedure involves submitting a formal request to speak at least 48 hours before the meeting time.

If your state mandates a public comment period but does not specify when it must occur, it is advisable to schedule it at the end of the meeting. This allows guests to become acquainted with the board members and with how the meetings are run. It also lets the board conduct previously scheduled work without getting derailed by public comment.

Give members of the public a limited amount of time in which to make their comments. Encourage them to put their comments in writing so that they can be submitted to trustees prior to the meeting.

 *Sample on page 53*

BEST PRACTICE TIP

Making Public Participation Productive

- Members of the public who want to speak at board meetings often want to lodge some kind of complaint. The school should have a very clear grievance policy. Most policies recommend dealing with the issues at the lowest possible level, bringing issues to the board only when resolution cannot be achieved under the CEO's direction. If the board must hear the grievance of an angry parent, it is wise to hear the parent out, and then tell the parent the board will respond within a certain amount of time. The board may need time to deliberate on the issue.

- Make sure you clearly understand your state's open meeting law. Most laws do not require an open public comment period, but many charter school boards mistakenly believe that they are legally required to allow public comment.

- Again, it is highly advised that any public comment be submitted ahead of time in writing to the board chair at least 48 hours before the board meeting. More often than not, issues raised by members of the public are not appropriate to be heard at the board meeting and should first be sent to the management team, instead.

4. Laws and Procedures

4.1. What is "open meeting law," and can we really be an effective board and comply with this law?

Open meeting laws (sometimes referred to as "sunshine laws") vary from state to state. In general, because charter schools are public schools, they must comply with their state's open meeting law. Typically, the law requires boards to hold open discussions regarding their actions (unless a specific exemption permits an executive session), inform the public of all meetings times, and keep accurate records of the proceedings.

Most charter school boards are unclear about how to comply with the open meeting law. *The most important thing is to understand the intent of the law but not to be paralyzed from doing good work because of it.* Remember that your board's composition is constantly changing, and people need periodic training and orientation around the law. Specific technical questions should be addressed to your board's legal counsel, but to get you going in the right direction, here are some general steps towards complying with the open meeting law:

1. Make sure that every board member and your CEO has a copy of the applicable open meeting law.

2. Include a discussion of compliance with the open meeting law as part of your new board member orientation.

3. Annually, provide the full board with a refresher on the open meeting law, and ask the board's legal counsel for guidance with specific questions.

4. Annually, ask the board's legal counsel to review your procedures for complying with the open meeting law. This review should include reviewing the board minutes, procedures for posting your meetings, and meeting protocols.

Again, remember the spirit of the law is that the public sees the board doing its work in public. Don't let that stop you from having open, honest, and difficult conversations. Let the public hear the tough questions you are asking and see the hard choices you are making as a charter school board.

The more everyone understands what it takes to deliver exceptional public education, the better off we all will be. Observing a public charter school board in action is an excellent way to educate interested members of the public. (See the "Open Meeting Law Quiz" in part II.)

⚖ 🗖 *Sample on page 49*

4.2. Do open meeting laws specify what needs to be in our minutes?

Possibly. Some states' open meeting laws have very specific requirements for board meeting minutes; others do not. Obviously, you should actually read the law and confirm that all specified requirements are present in your minutes. (Most laws are accessible online.) If there is any ambiguity in your mind, ask your board's legal counsel for guidance. Share your findings with the full board, and ensure that all trustees and especially the board secretary and the committee chairs understand the requirements.

BEST PRACTICE TIP

Open Meeting Law Quiz

Have your board take the Open Meeting Law Quiz, found in part II of this book. Your board's legal counsel should provide an answer key based on the specific requirements of your state.

Repeat this process every year (taking the key and having your legal counsel review the answers), to serve as a reminder, to make sure any new trustees are aware of the law's nuances, and to confirm that your answer key still conforms to any changes that might have been made in the law.

II *Sample on page 49*

4.3. If we don't have a quorum, should we cancel the meeting?

No! Except in rare circumstances, meetings should be held as scheduled. The only thing you can't do without a quorum is vote. Plenty of business can still be conducted. The first order of business should be to discuss the absentee rate and develop a strategy to address it.

BEST PRACTICE TIP

Keep on Schedule

Keep to your schedule as much as possible. Board members are volunteers and lead busy lives. It is more realistic to expect them to routinely attend board meetings if they know about them well in advance. Ideally, you should give the trustees all the board meeting and board retreat dates a year in advance. Many charter schools hold their board meetings during the third week of the month. This allows time to prepare the financial statements for a timely review by the board.

4.4. How should the board meeting be set up, physically?

Board members should be seated around a table. Seating should make it easy for members to see each other and be conducive to productive problem-solving and decision-making. Don't set the meeting up for an audience; set it up for the ease of the board members.

Ideally, name cards should identify each board member. This clarifies who is speaking to members of the public and other guests. It is also helpful to new members.

Members of the public, teachers, parents, students, and all other non-leadership staff members should sit away from the board table in seats clearly designated for observers.

The CEO and other senior staff (e.g., business manager, development director) should sit at the table with the board. Staff members should sit together so that they can pass written communications back and forth, if necessary. The CEO and board chair should also sit next to each other.

BEST PRACTICE TIP

Keep Meetings Formal

Remember, charter school board meetings are open to the public. Any member of the school community or the community at large can attend to see how decisions are made and how the taxpayers' money is spent. Get in the habit of making your board meetings relatively formal and professional. You may not have members of the public at every meeting, but you should run every meeting as if you had an audience.

4.5. Where should members of the public sit during board meetings?

Often, boards want to appear welcoming so they invite members of the public to sit at the table with the full board. This is not a good idea; it sends the wrong message about the role of the public. Members of the public are there to observe the board doing its business, not to interfere or weigh in on the board business, except at predetermined times. It is better to have a designated spot for members of the public to sit, which is slightly away from the full board.

4.6. What should a typical board meeting be like?

In general, unless there are extreme circumstances, board meetings should last no more than two hours.

They should begin and end on time. Charter schools are extremely fortunate to find trustees who believe in the school's mission and who are willing to give a substantial amount of their time to governing the school each month. Honor them by beginning and ending according to the scheduled time.

Meetings should be well facilitated, and the board should follow the agenda closely.

Every board meeting should be focused on dealing with at least one strategic, policy-level issue. Think carefully about how best to use the group's time. If the full board meets every month for two hours, that is only one full day a year! Board time is precious and should be used efficiently.

An advance packet of information should be sent out before every board meeting. Board members should come to the meetings having read the advanced materials, which typically provide background and context for the strategic issues to be discussed. Too much board time is wasted explaining facts and figures; providing these in advance allows the group to start the discussion with the same information so that they can focus on the strategic.

It is not necessary for each committee to report at each board meeting. They should report to the full board only if they have reached a conclusion to be shared with the board or if they wish to bring an issue to the board for a strategic discussion or vote. The same should apply to the CEO report.

BEST PRACTICE TIP

Strategy, Not Just Reporting

Avoid simply reporting during board meetings. Instead, committees should identify strategic issues and facilitate a board discussion around those issues.

4.7. What is an executive session? When does a board go into executive session?

Executive session means that the board adjourns to a closed-door session not open to the public. Only board members participate in executive session, although they may choose to ask the CEO, other staff, or special guests (such as their legal counsel) to attend.

The laws governing executive sessions vary from state to state, so be sure to understand your specific legal requirements. However, most laws typically require that:

- the board first convenes in open session
- the presiding officer of the board cites the reason for meeting in executive session
- a majority of board members vote to meet in executive session
- minutes must be taken and votes recorded during such a session, and records remain confidential only so long as publication may defeat the lawful purpose of the executive session.

Generally, under most state laws, charter school boards may hold executive session under limited circumstances, including:

- to discuss the reputation, character, or mental or physical health of an individual, but not his or her professional competence
- to consider discipline or dismissal of an employee, or hear complaints or charges brought against an employee (Note: If the board is meeting in executive session under either of these exceptions, the individual in question is afforded certain rights, including the right to have notice of the meeting, the right to be present, the right to have counsel attend, and the right to speak on his or her own behalf.)
- to discuss strategy relating to litigation or collective bargaining
- to consider the purchase or lease of real estate, if an open meeting would undermine the school's negotiating position
- to investigate charges of criminal misconduct or discuss the deployment of security devices
- when another law requires the board to meet in executive session, such as to protect the privacy of an individual.

5. Improving Discussion and Decision-Making

5.1. How can we make sure board meetings are strategic and not merely reactive?

When you create your board calendar (as described in 1.3), time your actions and deadlines in a way that will be most effective. Think about the natural flow of the board year, and pencil in items you know will need to be discussed in certain months (the annual audit, authorizer inspection, approval of the budget, CEO evaluation, officer elections, and so on). Then think of other pressing issues—succession planning, capital campaign plans, and so forth. List them all. Then prioritize them. Develop annual priorities, with assignments of accountability, and timeframes. Start plugging them into the calendar. When other issues arise, you can now weigh them against the already scheduled topics and decide what you might take off the agenda in order to discuss this new business.

▤ *Sample on page 42*

5.2. What are some strategies for improving our board meetings?[1]

1. **Set the context for issues and discussions.** Provide background information and historical perspective. Explain "how the organization got to this point." Outline the purpose of the discussion and define the desired outcomes—for example, to make a decision, to gather more information for a future vote, and so on. Use an agenda item cover sheet to help set the context. But at the meeting, set the context orally, as well.

   📖 *Sample on page 39*

2. **Distinguish between routine and strategic issues.** Focus on strategic dialogue and decision-making, not on reporting. Don't waste time on routine issues.

3. **Distinguish between governance and management.** Be clear, beforehand, what portion of the upcoming discussion is "governance" and what part is "management." A good rule of thumb is that the board focuses on defining results and the staff focuses on the means to achieve those results.

4. **Make sure that each person has the opportunity to speak, including every board member and the CEO.** The board chair or committee chair should not dominate the discussion, but should facilitate discussion by others. The board chair can do several things to ensure a productive meeting:

   • Facilitate the discussion and monitor participation.

   • Stop those who are inappropriately dominating the conversation and allow others to speak.

   • Move the discussion along by discouraging the repetition of similar comments; ask for a summary of key points to help move the board toward action.

   • Ask if the board is ready to vote.

---

1 Adapted from Simone P. Joyaux's work: www.simonejoyaux.com. Used with permission.

5. **The board chair should manage the meeting time and make sure that it is used well.** Remind the group of the time allocated for each item on the agenda. If time runs out, ask the group if it wishes to modify the agenda in order to have more time to discuss the topic, or if it wishes to end the discussion and move the agenda. Beware! Two hours per month in a board meeting is almost always sufficient time. If you are meeting more often or longer, take a look at what you are doing and how you are doing it.

6. **Monitor and question your own process.** Examine the topics you are talking about and decide if that's what you should be discussing. Use minimal parliamentary procedure to conduct business efficiently.

7. **Make sure the board accesses and uses relevant information for deliberation and decision-making.** Don't just look at your school in a vacuum. Make sure you are using contextual data. For example, if you are voting on an increased salary for your CEO, you should know how the proposed salary compares to other charter and district schools in your area.

8. **Make sure the board considers alternative actions** reflective of diverse points of view, hears all sides, and assesses the positive and negative consequences of various choices.

9. **Ask tough questions**, find areas of commonality, vote, and support the decision you finally make.

10. **If the board is planning to delegate work to a committee or task force**, it should first make sure the full board has approved the process and defined the parameters of the work.

5.3. Our board tries to use consensus decision-making. We talk and talk and talk until finally everyone agrees. Is this the right approach?

Consensus does not mean unanimity or total agreement. Neither does consensus guarantee that everyone gets his or her choice. However, each person must feel that they have had adequate opportunity to be heard. Each person in the group must believe that the decision was fair, even if they do not agree with the outcome. It is significant to note that once a decision has been made by the board, the entire board must support the decision to the broader community.

5.4. Our board always has unanimous decisions. Is this good?

No. Often, boards who state with pride that they have always had unanimous decisions lack the diversity of opinions and perspectives required to solve the challenges facing most charter schools.

5.5. Should we evaluate our board meetings?

Yes, there are a number of quick and easy ways to do this at the end of each board meeting.

Option 1: + – Δ (plus, minus, delta). Go around the room and ask trustees to weigh in on:

- \+   What was good about the meeting?

- –   What wasn't effective about the meeting?

- Δ   What would they change?

Option 2: Develop a quick set of standard questions, and rotate through the trustees, asking each one to comment. Sample questions:

- Was this an effective meeting?

- Why or why not?

- How could it have been improved?

- What percentage of our time was reactive vs. strategic? (See the chart "Strategic, Not Reactive" on page 17.)

5.6. I am frustrated with how our meetings are run, and I am not the chair of the board. What can I do to make our board meetings more efficient?

First of all, don't sit back and make the chair do all the hard work. Every board member is responsible for smooth-running board meetings, regularly attending, coming prepared, not dominating the conversation, and focusing the conversation on governance, not management.

Assess whether the chair is capable of fixing the problems you are observing. Is the chair a great facilitator of discussion, but has difficulty keeping the meeting on schedule? If so, make the suggestion that board members take turns being the timekeeper. Does the chair constantly need to redirect a board member with a personal agenda? Help the chair out and rein that person in as well.

Here are a few tips or group norms that may improve your board meetings. Consider asking each board member to agree to abide by the following:

1. Listen carefully. Ask tough questions, but don't do it for the sake of causing dissent.

2. Avoid simply repeating what others have said; it just wastes time.

3. Find patterns and commonalities, as well as differences. Explore the differences to find the best answer.

4. Don't focus your opinion and advocate for it. Instead, listen to the perspective of others, question your own assumptions, and bring it all together for the best answer.

5. Ask for focus from fellow trustees. Give feedback when you think others are not contributing to the effective functioning of the group.

6. Use parliamentary procedure to "call the question," if you feel that discussion has lasted too long. But use this tool carefully!

    Call the Question: End discussion and vote.

5.7. We have a hard time staying on topic during board meetings. What should we do?

First, you should have a clearly defined agenda that makes a reasonable guess at how long each topic should take. Every topic could take more time, but the board chair and the CEO should carefully weigh the time allotted for the board meeting and balance the time accordingly.

Then, you should honor the allotted time. If you are going over the designated time, the board chair should stop whoever is presenting and say, "We've only allotted fifteen minutes for this discussion. Do trustees feel we should continue the conversation, if so that will mean reducing the time for other items on the agenda?" Then let the full board weigh in on how to proceed.

BEST PRACTICE TIP

Keeping Time

Don't go over the allotted two-hour window. Train the board to become disciplined in how they use the group's time. Typically, two hours should be enough to complete the board's business.

Appoint a timekeeper. Sometimes the board chair can be a great facilitator but a lousy timekeeper. If this is the case with your board, ask someone to use a stopwatch and be the timekeeper. You could rotate through all the trustees with a different trustee being the timekeeper each month.

PART II. SAMPLES AND QUIZZES

The following example documents and policies are some of BoardOnTrack's most commonly requested examples. Our growing library includes hundreds of similar documents based on the best practices of some of the most effective charter school boards. For more samples and information about BoardOnTrack, visit www.boardontrack.com.

Agenda: June 19, 2014 at 6:30 P.M.

ABC Charter School Board Meeting

Agenda Item	Purpose	Who	Materials	Time
1. Minutes from 5-8-2014	Vote	Board Chair	Minutes from 5-8-2014	5 min
2. Facility				
A. Year 4+ Facility	Discussion	Facility Committee Chair	Site Search Summary	10 min

B. Year 3 Facility
   – Overview
   – Financing
	Vote	Facility Committee Chair	3-Year Facility Summary document	20 min

3. Finances				
A. Monthly Financial Update	Discussion	Finance Committee Chair	April, May, June Budget to Actual	5 min
B. Final Year 3	Vote	Finance Committee Chair	Budget/ Summary of Key Changes	20 min
4. Board Expansion				
• New Board Members	Input	Governance Committee Chair	2 board candidate résumés	10 min
5. Development				
• Fundraising Update – Increasing Next Year's Goal	Input	Development Committee Chair	Prospect Worksheet for homework	10 min
6. Executive Session				
• CEO Salary Review	Vote	Board Chair	CEO Salary Review Memo	20 min
7. Housekeeping				10 min
• Next Board Meeting – Board Retreat	Discussion	Board Chair	Draft topics in packet, Draft dates & outcomes	10 min
8. Adjournment	Vote			

(Next Board Meeting: July 17, 2014 from 6:00 P.M. to 8:00 P.M.)

 *www.boardontrack.com*

Agenda Item Cover Sheet

Agenda Item:	New Board Members
Purpose:	For board vote
Submitted by:	M. Candler, S. Hansen

Background

- Board Candidate Tom Freeman (see résumé attached)
- Mr. Freeman was referred to the school by a professional associate of J. Zoia
- Mr. Freeman visited the school on 3-28-2014 and met with R. Smith, J. Hirsch, J. Zoia and a student
- T. Freeman also discussed board candidacy with Marci Cornell-Feist via phone on 5-2-2014
- Mr. Freeman would bring several great strengths to the board including:
  - Extensive financial experience
  - Access to financial resources
  - Startup experience
  - Recruiting and leading teams
  - Long-term strategy development
- In addition, Mr. Freeman is very enthusiastic about serving on the board. He recently finished an intensive MBA program at Wharton while working full time and he now has time and energy to give to a new endeavor. Mr. Freeman is looking for something that will be fulfilling, and give him a different sense of accomplishment than his work in the corporate sector. Mr. Freeman seems to really understand our charter school model, was very inspired by seeing how eager our kids are to learn, has the time commit to board work, and asked great questions about the school, sustainability etc.

Recommendation

We recommend a motion be made to nominate Mr. Freeman as a Trustee of ABC Charter School.

Minutes: May 8, 2014

A meeting of the board of trustees (the "board") of ABC Charter School (the "school") was held on May 8, 2014 at 6 P.M. at the school.

The following members of the board were present:

M. Beneke, R. Bollinger, M. Candler, M. Cowan, E. Evans, S. Hansen, C. Kearney, R. Moran, A. Perkins
Robert Stevens (CEO) and Sarah Jones (Principal) were also present.

Board members absent:

W. Vaneski (Notified)

1. **Minutes of Previous Meeting**
   The board:
   VOTED
   To approve the draft minutes of the last board meeting held on April 3, 2014, in the form previously circulated.

2. **Management Update**
   Mr. Stevens provided a management update on recruitment efforts, budget, and real estate issues.

3. **Renovation**
   After discussion, the board:
   VOTED
   To approve the $140,000 renovation of the first floor of the current building to provide expansion space for the school.

4. **Enrollment**
   Mr. Stevens led a discussion of a proposed seventh-grader enrollment policy, which will be a revision to the enrollment policy currently set forth in the school's charter. The board:
   VOTED
   To approve the Enrollment Policy prepared by Mr. Stevens substantially in the form distributed to the board at the meeting, and to authorize Mr. Stevens to submit said policy to the Department of Education for approval.

5. **Consulting Agreement**
   Mr. Stevens next presented the board with a consulting agreement for Mr. George Jacoby, with respect to work related to the acquisition of a permanent location for the school. After a brief

discussion the board:

VOTED

To approve the consulting agreement by and between the School and Mr. George Jacoby.

There being no further business to be transacted, and upon motion duly made, seconded and approved, the meeting was adjourned at 8:10 P.M.

Respectfully Submitted,

———————————————

Rachel Bollinger, Secretary

Attendance 2013–14 School Year

Trustee	11 Jul	29 Aug	12 Sep	3 Oct	14 Nov	Board Retreat	12 Dec	9 Jan	13 Feb	13 Mar	3 Apr	8 May	19 Jun
M. Beneke	•	•	N	•	•	•	•	•	•	•	•	•	
R. Bollinger	•	•	N	•	•	•	•	•	•	•	•	•	
M. Candler	•	•	•	•	•	•	•	•	•	•	•	•	
M. Cowan	•	U	•	U	•	U	U	U	•	U	U	•	
E. Evans	•	•	•	•	•	•	•	•	•	•	•	•	
S. Hansen	•	•	•	•	•	•	•	•	•	•	•	•	
C. Kearney	•	•	•	•	•	•	•	•	•	•	•	•	
R. Moran	•	N	•	•	•	•	•	•	•	•	•	•	
A. Perkins	•	•	•	•	•	•	•	•	•	•	•	•	
W. Vaneski	•	•	•	•	•	N	•	•	•	•	•	•	N
Staff													
R. Stevens (CEO)	•	•	•	•	•	•	•	•	•	•	•	•	
S. Jones (Principal)	•	•	•	•	•	•	•	•	•	•	•	•	

• Present   N Notified absence   U Un-notified absence

www.boardontrack.com

Board Calendar: 2013–2014 School Year

Date	Activity/Agenda Items
July 11, Monday (6:00 P.M. – 8:00 P.M.)	Board meeting • Revised budget • Auditor selection • Test data • Committees and board calendars
August 29, Monday (5:00 P.M. – 8:00 P.M.)	Back-to-school picnic (meet families and staff) from 5 P.M. – 6 P.M. Board meeting, 6 P.M. – 8 P.M. • Annual financial statement • Board position descriptions • Committee descriptions • Board calendar approval
September 12, Monday (6:00 P.M. – 8:00 P.M.)	Board meeting • Accountability plan • Annual report for authorizer • Revised board calendar • Board position descriptions • Division of labor among board members
October 3, Monday (6:00 P.M. – 8:00 P.M.)	Board meeting/working session • Working session: strategic plan preparation and outreach strategies
October 16, Sunday (1:00 P.M. – 3:00 P.M.)	Board/staff get-together sponsored by board and administration
November 5, Saturday (9:00 A.M. – 3:00 P.M.)	All-day board retreat • Focus on strategic planning

Date	Activity/Agenda Items
November 14, Monday (6:00 P.M. – 8:00 P.M.)	Board meeting • Quarterly financial statements • Possible development training session (if so, meeting might run from 6 P.M. – 9 P.M. to allow for a 2-hour session)
December 12, Monday (6:00 P.M. – 8:00 P.M.)	Board meeting/working session • Working session: implementing strategic plan and focus on development
January 9, Monday (6:00 P.M. – 8:00 P.M.)	Board meeting
February 13, Monday (6:00 P.M. – 8:00 P.M.)	Board meeting/working session • Working session: implementing strategic plan and focus on development
March 13, Monday (6:00 P.M. – 8:00 P.M.)	Board meeting
March 22, Wednesday (8:30 A.M. – 12:30 P.M.)	Board Members Come to School Day
April 3, Monday (6:00 P.M. – 8:00 P.M.)	Board meeting/working session • Working session: strategic planning for 2014–2015
May 8, Monday (6:00 P.M. – 8:00 P.M.)	Board meeting • Quarterly financial statements • Officer nomination process

Date	Activity/Agenda Items
June 13, Tuesday (5:00 P.M. – 9:00 P.M.)	Community showcase (students demonstrating what they have learned); Annual board meeting <ul><li>CEO evaluation (discussion only open to board members)</li><li>Selection of new board members</li><li>Election of officers</li></ul>

Note: A second board retreat may be scheduled in the summer. In addition, we may try to schedule a board training session on development during the school year.

General Notes

- All meetings will be held at ABC Charter School unless otherwise indicated.
- All meetings will be held on Mondays, unless otherwise indicated.
- All meetings will be held from 6:00 P.M. to 8:00 P.M., unless otherwise indicated.
- We are making an attempt to have a full board meeting every month. We will alternate meetings focusing on issues of oversight with meetings focusing on deeper discussion that include a very short "board business section" (20 minutes or less), freeing up the remaining time for deeper strategy topics. Recommended topics are listed above.
- Any materials that the board needs to review for decision-making or discussion purposes must be provided to the board chair at least one week prior to the board meeting. All materials related to agenda items will be distributed as a package for board review. (Note: If something is proposed that is not placed on the agenda, the decision will be discussed with the board member who suggested the item to determine how best to handle it.)
- Draft agendas will be distributed one week after the prior meeting. Any suggested changes to the agenda must be made by 48 hours after distribution.
- Board calendar will be updated periodically to reflect new information.

Board Attendance Policy

Purpose

This policy was developed with the recognition that board membership is voluntary and that individual members contribute their time and energy in different ways. However, because board meetings are the only forum during which the board can discuss and vote on major school policies and decisions, attendance at these meetings carries a special importance. All board members will receive a copy of this policy to ensure that everyone is properly informed about the expectations for board attendance.

Definitions

"Notified" Absence: For an absence to be a "notified" absence, a board member must notify the person running the meeting (usually the chair or vice-chair) by 12:00 P.M. the day of the meeting that he or she will be absent.

"Un-notified" Absence: For an absence to be an "un-notified" absence, a board member failed to notify the person running the meeting (usually the chair or vice-chair) by 12:00 P.M. the day of the meeting that he or she will be absent.

Board Attendance Problem

If any of the following conditions exist, it is considered a board attendance problem:

1. The member has two absences in a row, whether notified or unnotified.
2. The member misses one third of the total number of board meetings during one of their term years.

Process for Responding to a Board Attendance Problem

The board secretary will keep track of board member attendance through the board meeting minutes and will provide this information to the chair. The chair will directly contact a board member who is at risk of potentially violating the policy to issue both a verbal and written warning as well as discuss the problem. If a board member does violate the policy, the chair will bring this to the attention of the board for discussion, after which point a majority vote will be held to determine possible termination from the board.

Secretary Job Description

Member of and Elected by: The board of trustees
Reports to: The chair and the board of trustees
Supports: Member of the staff or volunteer taking minutes
Term of Office: One year; renewable for three consecutive years

General Responsibilities

Provides direction for the keeping of legal documents including minutes of all meetings of the board of the school.

Specific Responsibilities

1. Certify and keep at the principal office of the corporation the original or a copy of the bylaws as amended or otherwise altered to date.
2. Keep at the principal office of the corporation or at such a place as the board may determine a book of minutes of all meetings of the trustees and meetings of committees. Minutes shall record time and place of meeting, whether regular or special, how called, how notice was given, the names of those present or represented at the meeting, and the proceedings thereof.
3. Present for approval by the board copies of all minutes of meetings of the board.
4. Ensure that all notices are duly given in accordance with the provisions of the bylaws or as required by law.
5. In general, serve as the protocol officer of the board, ensuring that the keeping and posting of meeting minutes, meeting notifications, adherence to open meeting laws, and other procedural requirements are followed legally and ethically.
6. In general, perform all duties incident to the office of the clerk and such other duties as may be required by law, by the Articles of Incorporation or bylaws, or which may be assigned to him or her from time to time by the board of trustees.
7. Recognize his or her responsibility to set the example for other board members by contributing financially at a level that is meaningful to him or her and by playing a major role in fundraising activities.

Qualifications

- A commitment to the school and an understanding of the school and its values, mission and goals, and the distinctions between governance and management
- An understanding of the required record keeping and the laws of the jurisdiction (city, state) in which the school operates
- A capacity for attention to detail

Indicators of Effectiveness

- Meets annual goals as identified and adopted by the board at the beginning of the leadership term
- Is perceived by other board members as being an accurate and reasonable steward of the decision-making history of the organization and as being ever mindful of the duties and requirements of public service
- Is perceived by staff as supporting and adding value to their work
- Is perceived by a majority of parents and other community members as being accessible, fair, constructive, and representative of the interests of the broader school community

 www.boardontrack.com

Open Meeting Law Quiz

Distribute this pop quiz to the full board once a year at a board
meeting. Ask trustees and senior staff to complete it on the spot.
Then tally the results and discuss. Have copies of the open meeting
law on hand and double-check your answers together. Ideally, ask your
legal counsel to give you an "answer key" prior to asking the full board
to complete this exercise.

⚖️ 🖥️ *www.boardontrack.com*

	Yes	No	Don't Know
1. Does your state have an open meeting law?			
2. Does your open meeting law allow board meetings to be held by speakerphone?			
3. Does your open meeting law permit board members to vote by speakerphone?			
4. Does your open meeting law apply to committee meetings?			
5. Do you know the requirements for giving notice of public meetings—where to post and how far in advance?			
6. Does your law require you to post committee meetings?			
7. Does your law require you to take minutes in a particular way?			
8. Do you understand under what circumstances your board can go into executive session?			
9. Do you review the open meeting law as a group annually?			
10. Does the board's legal counsel review your compliance with the open meeting law annually?			
11. Does the board secretary review open meeting law compliance monthly?			

Board Meetings Quiz

Have your full board and senior staff take this quiz at a board
meeting, tally the results, and then discuss them as a group. Consider
how you are doing, discuss how to become better, and prioritize the
action steps that will help you to improve. Aspire to be able to answer
"yes" to all of these.

	Yes	No	Don't Know
1. We have an active engaged board evidenced by typically having all board members in attendance at each board meeting.			
2. We always comply with the Open Meeting Law.			
3. Our board meetings always start and end on time.			
4. Our meetings are well facilitated by the chair.			
5. We rarely have members of the public attend our board meetings.			
6. Our CEO and board chair partner to shape the board meeting agendas and the overall work of the board for the year.			
7. We have lively discussions and occasional dissent.			
8. Our board focuses on results, guided by a clear set of measurable board-level and management-level goals for the year.			
9. An advance packet goes out ahead of time to set the stage for strategic conversations.			
10. We spend most of our board meeting time discussing strategic issues rather than reporting on items that have already happened.			

Observing Board Meetings

An excellent way to improve your board meetings is to go watch another board in action. Identify another charter school in your community (or another non-profit board if you prefer) and observe one of their meetings.

Although charter school board meetings are open to the public, it is generally good practice to call the CEO ahead of time and let them know that you plan to attend the board meeting as an observer.

You will probably get a lot more out of the meeting if you request the agendas and minutes from the last few meetings, and read them ahead of time. These are public documents, so it is fine to request them. By looking at them ahead of time, you will get a context for the meeting you are about to observe.

I recommend going early (20 minutes or so). You can learn a lot by introducing yourself to people ahead of time and also by watching the setup/group dynamics, etc.

The following are questions that you should answer and things to look for when you observe a board meeting.

Logistics

1. Where was the meeting held? What was the room like?
2. What was the seating setup like? Was it a comfortable atmosphere? Why or why not?
3. Where did the CEO sit?
4. Where did the board sit?
5. Where did other staff members sit?
6. Where did you and other members of the public sit?
7. What would you have done differently as far as logistics?

Participation

1. Who attended the meeting? List their names and roles.
2. Who was absent? How many people? Why?
3. Did the meeting start on time? Was everyone there on time?
4. Who facilitated the meeting?
5. How would you characterize the facilitation?

6. Who spoke at the meeting? Did everyone? A few people? Did one person dominate?
7. What was the CEO's role?
8. Did anyone from the public speak or make comments?
9. Was there anyone in the audience?
10. What would you have done differently as far as the participation?

Meeting Content

1. Was there a meeting agenda?
2. Did the meeting keep to the agenda? Why or why not?
3. Did it run for the scheduled amount of time? Longer or shorter? Why?
4. Think about what you know about governance and management. Did the board meeting focus more on governance or management?
5. What substantive discussions did the board have? Do you think these were appropriate discussions for the board level?
6. What major decisions were made? How were the decisions made?
7. Was it possible to tell if the board had working committees? Was it evident whether or not the committees had done work in between meetings?
8. What would you have done differently about the meeting content?

CEO's Role

1. What role did the CEO play in the board meeting?
2. How much did they speak?
3. What role did they play in decision-making?
4. What did you surmise about their relationship with their board?
5. If you were in their shoes, what would you have done differently?

Final Thoughts

1. What was the most important thing that you learned by attending this board meeting?
2. What additional questions do you have about boards and board meetings?
3. Ask the CEO to send you a copy of the minutes when they are complete. Do the minutes accurately reflect the meeting you attended?

Public Comment Procedures

What follows is a sample public meetings comment procedures document.

Many charter school boards have found it helpful to print this out on laminated cards and hand to any members of the public that attend a board meeting.

Welcome to ABC Charter School's board meeting. We appreciate your interest and involvement in making our school a success.

For your convenience, we have outlined below ABC's protocol for public comment and participation during our board meetings.

1. **Meetings**
   a. We welcome the public to all of our meetings
   b. ABC adheres to all of the requirements of the Open Meeting Act. *"The purpose and clearly stated intent of the Open and Public Meetings Act is to ensure that actions of the state are conducted openly and that the people's business is done in full view of the public."* The intent is that you can watch the public charter school board conducting its business, not that you weigh in at every juncture.
2. **Seating**
   a. Board members, ABC Charter School senior staff, and the CEO are invited to sit at the board table.
   b. A public seating area is provided for parents, teachers, and other guests.
3. **Public Comments**
   • For concerns or comments that the public wishes to have addressed during the board meeting, please submit them in writing to board@ABCCharterSchool.org 48 hours in advance of the meeting. The board chair will consider those items for inclusion on the next board meeting agenda, and you will be notified 24 hours in advance of the meeting whether the item will be included.

Thank you for attending our board meeting.

Board Effectiveness Quiz

Is your charter school board effective? Take this quiz, and see how you do.

	Yes	No	Don't Know
1. I know the key charter promises we have made to our authorizer and our community.			
2. I know how we measure these charter promises.			
3. We have a job description that details the roles and responsibilities of the full board.			
4. We have individual performance expectations for trustees that are written down and hold each board member accountable to these.			
5. Our board is large enough to have several active, well-functioning committees, who dive into substantive strategic issues and bring information back to the full board for further discussion and decision-making.			
6. Our board consistently demonstrates a clear understanding of the difference between governance and management.			
7. Our CEO actively helps create and shape effective governance.			
8. We have a strong partnership with our CEO that is built on mutual trust and respect.			
9. We have an effective process for evaluating, communicating with and supporting our CEO.			
10. Our board meetings are always well attended by our trustees.			

	Yes	No	Don't Know
11. We have a system in place to deal with chronic non-attending and underperforming board members.			
12. We review financials monthly and every board member has a firm grasp on the school's financial health.			
13. The majority of our board meeting time focuses on strategic issues rather than reporting on past events.			
14. Our organization uses academic achievement data to make decisions and improve results.			
15. Our board has formal tools and measures in place to measure overall organizational performance (finance, operations, staff retention, etc.).			
16. Each year the board establishes strategic board-level goals, articulating how the board will add value, that are specific and measurable.			
17. Our board spends most of its time setting the stage/creating the future rather than reacting and responding to immediate needs.			
18. Our board conducts an annual performance appraisal of the full board and of individual trustees.			
19. Annually, there is 100% board giving to the best of personal ability to the school's fundraising efforts.			
20. We have a succession plan for both board and school leadership.			

www.boardontrack.com

About the Author

Marci Cornell-Feist is among the most accomplished national experts on charter school governance. She has worked with over 500 charter schools nationwide to improve their effectiveness. She founded the charter school consultancy Meetinghouse Solutions in 2001, and has focused on charter school governance since the mid 1990s. After working with her first 200+ charter schools, she created BoardOnTrack to implement the most effective strategies and practices of her many clients, and as a means of spreading this information to a wider audience of charter schools.

Marci is author of the book *Board Meetings: A Guide for Charter Schools* and numerous articles, including two issue briefs for the National Association of Charter School Authorizers. Marci is also a co-founder of The Achievement Network, which helps schools use data-driven strategies to increase student achievement.

Earlier in her career, Marci worked throughout the nonprofit sector, including positions as a senior staffer at the Massachusetts Charter School Resource Center, Northwest Regional Director for the Student Conservation Association, Deputy Director of the Consortium/UNHCR refugee resettlement program in Lao P.D.R., and Peace Corps Volunteer in Thailand. Marci is a graduate of the Harvard Graduate School of Education and Bowdoin College.

BoardOnTrack

Your charter school is a multi-million dollar public enterprise.

Running it with untrained volunteers is a daunting task.

BoardOnTrack will help to leverage the efforts of your volunteer board members into real results: academic excellence and organizational sustainability.

We can help your board become more effective and efficient.

- ✓ In-depth analysis of your board's needs and goals
- ✓ Tools to manage your board's work and documents
- ✓ The training and materials your board needs most, when you need them
- ✓ Governance support and training for your school's leader

All tools and strategies have been road-tested with 200+ charter school boards nationwide, in 20+ different states.

Become a Member Today!

Structure Your Board

for **Success**

The right board structure provides the scaffolding for great governance to happen.

The wrong structure can cause harm. This book answers the most commonly asked questions about charter school board structure and gives you actionable steps to set up your board for optimal success.

100 pages, $15.95. Available at:
www.boardontrack.com/resources